USBORI YOUNG PUZZLE ADVENTURE STORIES

Lucy and the Sea Monster to the Rescue

Land of the Lost Teddies

Molly's Magic Carpet

Series Editor: Gaby Waters
Editor: Michelle Bates
Designers: Lucy Parris and Maria Wheatley

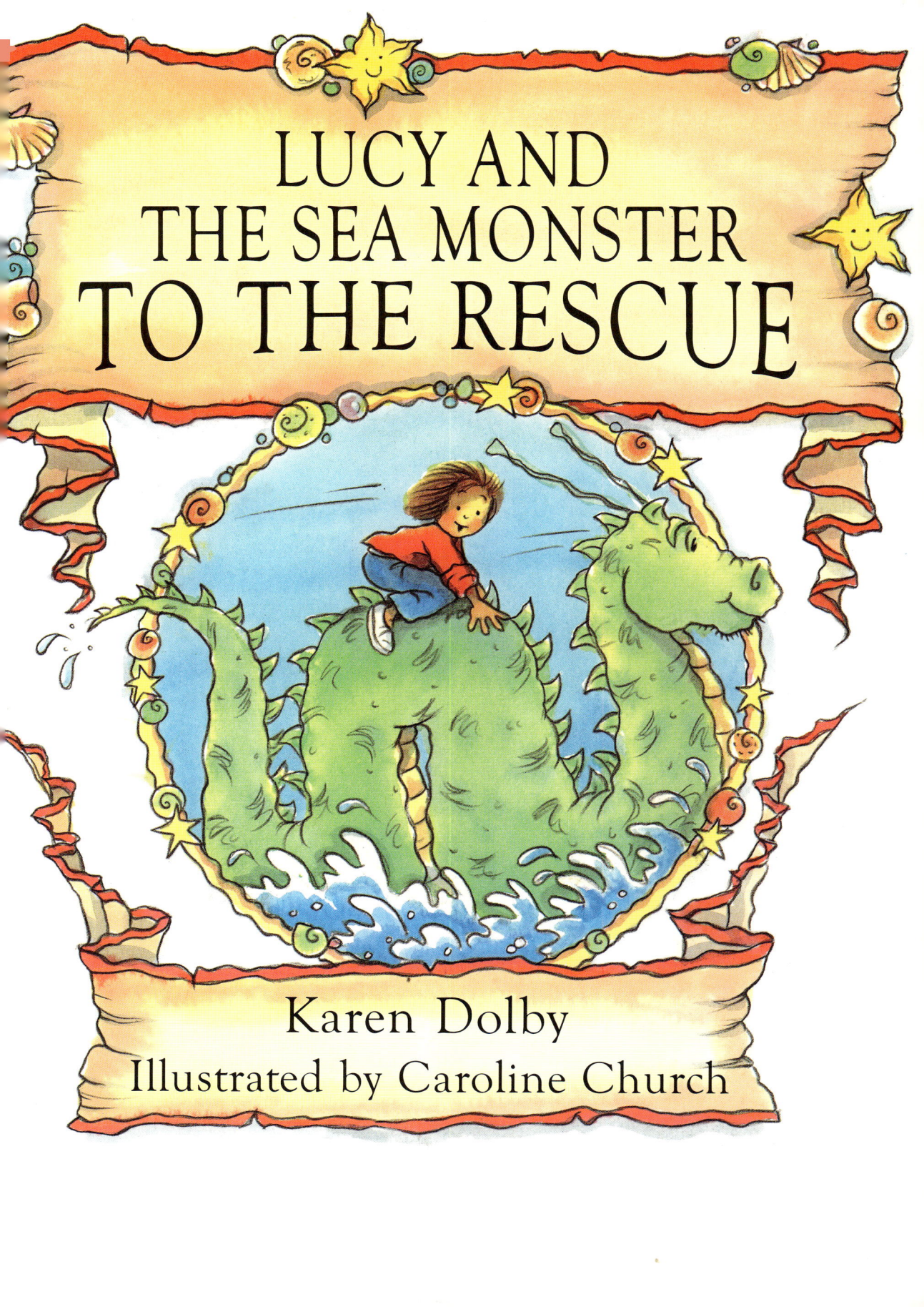

LUCY AND THE SEA MONSTER
TO THE RESCUE

Karen Dolby
Illustrated by Caroline Church

Contents

- 3   About this Book
- 4   Message in a Bottle
- 6   The Adventure Begins
- 8   Which Way?
- 10 Neptuna
- 12 Rory's News
- 14 Penguin Islands
- 16 The Pirates' Lair
- 18 Chocolate Island
- 20 Lucy on the Lookout
- 22 Sea Storm
- 24 A Safe Shelter
- 26 A Tricky Crossing
- 28 To the Rescue
- 30 Homeward Bound

About this Book

Lucy was scuffing through the pebbles on the beach waiting for something exciting to happen.

She did not have long to wait. When she looked up she saw a dot in the water coming closer. It was Horace, her sea monster friend.

Keep your eyes open for clues. If you get stuck, there are answers on pages 31 and 32.

Message in a Bottle

"Horace!" Lucy yelled, jumping up and down, waving wildly. She could hardly wait for him to reach the shore.

Horace and Lucy spent a happy morning playing hide and seek along the beach. Horace dipped and dived into rock pools, hiding below the water, then popping up again to splash Lucy unexpectedly.

Lucy watched a large bottle bobbing up and down until a big wave flung it onto the sand at her feet. How exciting! There was a note inside. Lucy uncorked the bottle and unrolled the paper. It was a message... a message from her friends, Mel and Jim.

Help!
We're stranded on Treasure Island!
Please come quickly
Mel and Jim

The Adventure Begins

"What are we waiting for? Let's go!" exclaimed Horace. Lucy scrambled onto his back and they were off.

Horace's coils sliced through the choppy sea. They whizzed along with Lucy's hair streaming behind.

Suddenly Horace stopped, so suddenly that Lucy almost fell off.

"What's wrong?" she asked.

"I'm not sure where Treasure Island is," he said. "It could be this way, that way or over there."

"We need help," said Lucy.

"You're right," said Horace. "Let's go to Neptuna, where the Merpeople live. They'll know where Treasure Island is."

Look at the signs on the rocks. Which way do you think they should go to find the Merpeople?

8

Which Way?

It was not long before they hit another problem. Their way was blocked.

"Oh no," sighed Lucy. "We'll never find Treasure Island or rescue Mel and Jim at this rate."

"Don't worry," said Horace. "I can see a path through the maze of rocks."

Can you find a safe way through the maze?

Neptuna

Lucy had never seen anything like Neptuna before. She rubbed her eyes to make sure she was not dreaming.

"It's market day," Horace said. "Everyone has come to do their shopping."

It was only then that Lucy noticed the floating stalls. They were piled high with shining shells, pretty pearls and coral combs; others sold fantastical fruits, fresh fish and delicious desserts.

"Let's see if anyone knows where Treasure Island is," said Lucy.

But no one did.

"Why don't you ask Rory, our roving reporter," a merman called Martin suggested. "Rory is always out and about on the lookout for news. He knows everything. He's easy to spot. He has binoculars around his neck and carries a notebook."

Can you spot Rory?

Rory's News

"Treasure Island?" said Rory, shaking his head. "Well there's good news and bad news. It's easy to spot. There are three pointed mountains, with a tree at the top of the middle one. But there's nothing to eat or drink, and it's a long way away, through the chilly Penguin Islands and beyond."

Lucy thought she had heard the bad news, but there was worse to come.

"You'd better watch out," said Rory. "Captain Silver and his pirates are heading for Treasure Island too."

Horace shivered. There was no time to lose. He knew those mean pirates only too well. They loved treasure and worst of all, kidnapped castaways to work on their ship.

Just then, Lucy glanced out to sea and spied something that made her shiver too.

What has Lucy spotted?

Penguin Islands

As the pirate ship sailed away into the distance, Lucy and Horace set off for the Penguin Islands. Penguins love ice and cold, and Lucy and Horace were about to discover just how cold and icy the islands really were. It grew chillier and chillier and as the ice lands came into view, snow began to fall.

Horace had to navigate his way between the icy islands. The penguins slid and slipped, splashing into the freezing water. But Horace was in trouble. It was hard to see through the snowflakes and even harder to steer between the jagged ice blocks, flying penguins and huge whales barring their way.

Can you find a clear route through the icy islands?

The Pirates' Lair

Horace and Lucy were happy to leave the icy Penguin Islands behind. The air grew warmer and the sun began to shine.

They swam swiftly on until they saw an island in the distance. Could this be Treasure Island? Horace was full of hope as he swam ashore, but they were in for a nasty surprise.

Not far away they heard voices and the sounds of people shouting. A horrid, burning smell filled the air. Peering through the trees Horace and Lucy spied pirates! They seemed to be squabbling about their supper.

"Yikes! This isn't Treasure Island," whispered Horace. "This is Booty Island, the pirates' base. I can see Red Reg Rover, Short Tom Gold, Black Beard and Peg Pinafore."

Can you work out which pirate is which?

I left you in charge of the food, Reg.

It's not my fault, I told Black Beard to watch the pot.

The sooner we catch some castaways to cook for us, the better.

Chocolate Island

Horace and Lucy didn't wait to hear more. Not wanting to be discovered, they slipped away silently.

Horace swam low in the water and Lucy lay almost flat on his back so the pirates would not spot them.

They needn't have worried, the pirates were far too busy arguing to notice anything going on around them.

It was not long before a large island loomed ahead. As they drew near, the tutti-frutti trees, chocolate pebbles and a chocolate fudge stream left Lucy in no doubt. This must be the famous Chocolate Island. Lucy licked her lips as a mouthwatering smell of chocolate hit her nose.

"We could take some food and drink for Mel and Jim," said Lucy.

"But how would we carry it?" asked Horace.

Can you find something to put the food and drink in?

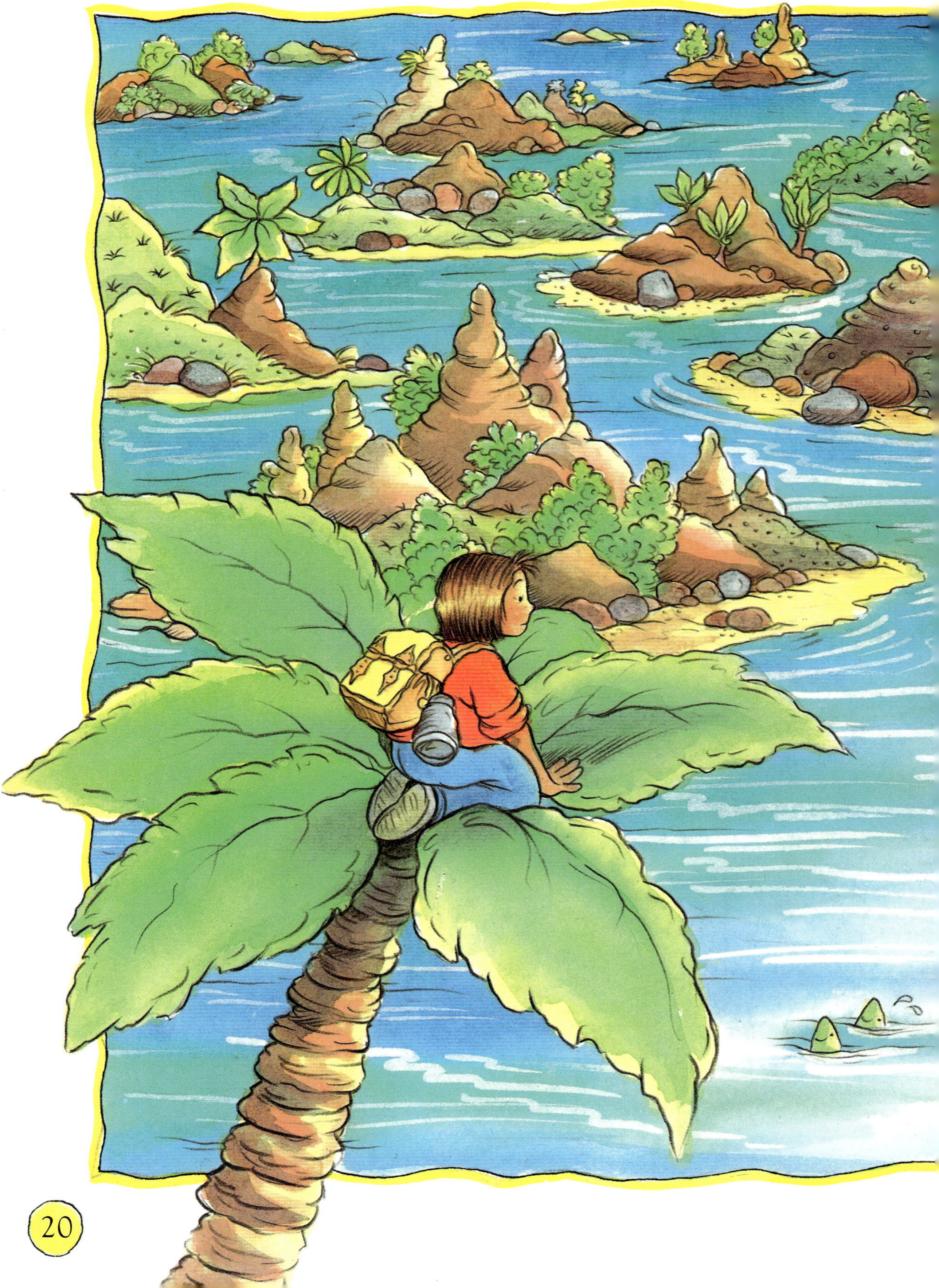

Lucy on the Lookout

They had soon filled their beaker and stashed all the food in the backpack. The sun was sinking low in the sky.

"We must be off," said Horace to Lucy. "I can see islands ahead. One of them must be Treasure Island. If you climb to the top of a tree you should be able to see which it is. It has three pointed mountains with a tree on top of the middle one."

Can you spot Treasure Island?

Sea Storm

No sooner had they set off, than a blustery wind began to blow. Before long it was whipping up the waves and blasting Lucy and Horace. It was hard for Lucy to keep her hold on Horace's back. The sky grew dark and menacing. Soon sharp, icy rain began to hail down on them.

"It's no good, we can't keep going," Horace yelled above the sound of the wind and waves. "We'll have to find somewhere to shelter from the storm."

Can you find a safe hiding place?

23

A Safe Shelter

Safe and dry in their cave, Lucy and Horace watched the rain lash down and lightning zigzag across the heavy, cloudy sky. A loud booming clap of thunder made Lucy jump but she soon spotted something which really made her heart pound.

What has Lucy seen?

There was no doubt. It was the pirates' ship and it was heading for Treasure Island. With the strong, gusting wind blowing the sails, it was speeding along. The pirates would reach the island in no time.

"What can we do?" cried Lucy. "We have to rescue Mel and Jim before the pirates arrive. There's no time to lose."

"Hop on my back," said Horace. "I have an idea."

A Tricky Crossing

The wind was dropping as Lucy and Horace put to sea once more.

"Our only hope is to take the short route to Treasure Island," said Horace. "But it is tricky and very dangerous."

Can you find a way through to Treasure Island? Beware the sharp rocks, sharks, crocodiles and lurking creatures.

27

To the Rescue

The dangerous shortcut had been worth it. When they reached Treasure Island, Lucy looked back out to sea. There was the pirates' ship. They had beaten the greedy band.

The pirates were really quite a lazy bunch and without the wind they were having to use oars. They were rowing very slowly and singing songs about treasure and gold. They had no idea that anyone else was on the island until a shout rang out.

"Land ahoy!" the lookout yelled, pointing his telescope at the island. "Bothering barnacles! We've been beaten to the loot! Enemy ahead!"

Lucy was happy to see Mel and Jim on the shore. They were smiling, holding up a large chest. What could be inside?

Mel and Jim looked horrified as the pirates began to row frantically fast to the island.

"There's room for us all on Horace's back," Lucy called.

Before they tied on the chest, Lucy could not resist taking a peep inside. She lifted the lid. This was no ordinary treasure and certainly not the kind of gold the pirates had been expecting.

But Horace was thrilled. "It's the ancient, magical statue of Marlin! It was stolen from our underwater palace," he exclaimed. "And we thought it was lost forever."

Lucy, Mel and Jim looked puzzled, but only for a moment.

Does the statue remind you of anyone?

Homeward Bound

With the pirates in hot pursuit, Horace set off. He zipped through the water, avoiding the sharp rocks, going as fast as he dared. At last they reached clear water. But where were the pirates? Had they escaped their greedy clutches?

Lucy, Horace, Mel and Jim looked back anxiously. They had no need to fear. With their eyes on the treasure and not on the rocks, the pirates had run their boat aground. There was a large hole in it. They were angrily splashing around, squabbling loudly and blaming one another.

"I don't think they will be bothering us again," smiled Lucy as they set off for home.

Answers

Pages 6-7
Can you find the mermaid drawn on the rock? It is just behind Horace. The arrow shows which direction they should take.

Pages 8-9
The safe route through the maze is marked here.

Pages 10-11
Rory is here.

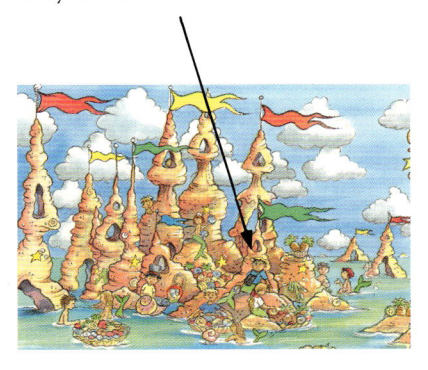

Pages 12-13
Lucy has spotted a skull and crossbones pirate flag. She is worried that this is the pirate ship Rory just told them about.

Pages 14-15
Lucy and Horace's way through the ice is shown here.

Pages 16-17
Did you guess who each pirate was from their name?

Red Reg Rover
Black Beard
Short Tom Gold
Peg Pinafore

Pages 18-19
Here are the backpack and beaker.

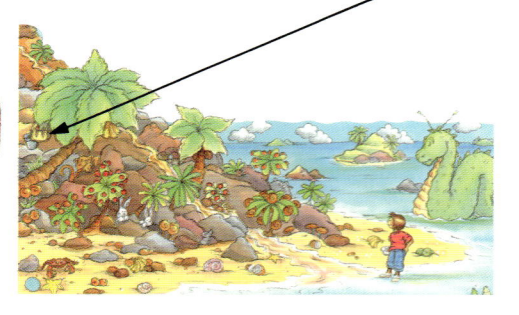

Pages 20-21
Treasure Island is here.

Pages 22-23
They can hide in the cave circled below. It will protect them from the storm and it is the only one which does not have a creature lurking inside.

Pages 24-25
Lucy has seen the pirate flag and ship sailing on.

Pages 26-27
Their route to Treasure Island is marked here.

Pages 28-29
The treasure is a gold sea monster's head. Does it remind you of Horace?

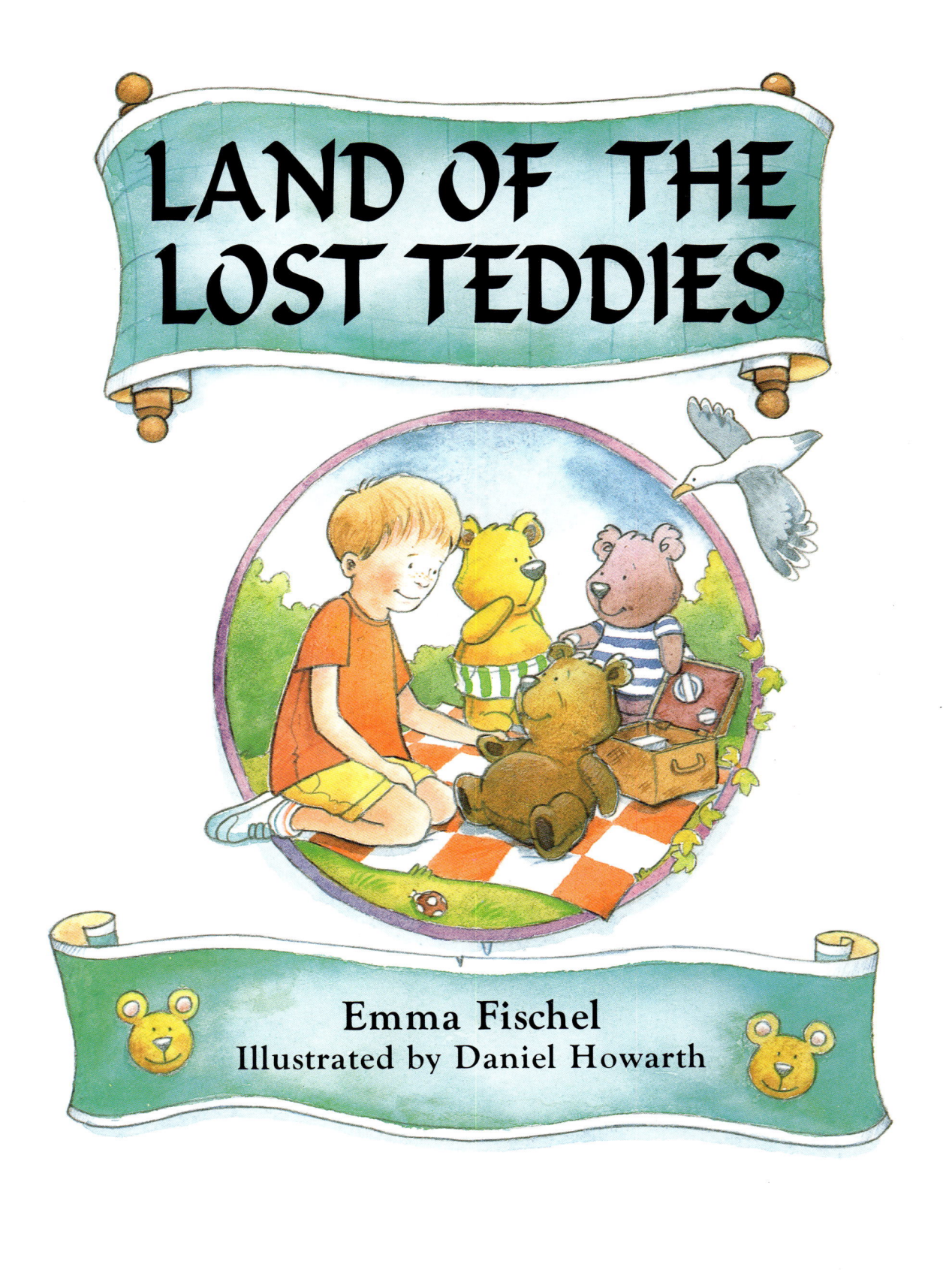

LAND OF THE LOST TEDDIES

Emma Fischel
Illustrated by Daniel Howarth

Contents

35	Getting Ready
36	Where's Teddy?
38	The Search Begins
40	On the Way
42	Which Way Now?
44	Picnic Path
46	Teddy Bears' Picnic
48	Bear Trouble
50	The Bear Cave
52	By the Lake
54	Mermaid Island
56	Another Clue
58	Bedtime Story
60	Teddy's Story
62	Homeward Bound
63	Answers

Getting Ready

Wilfie and his teddy, Eddie, are getting ready for an exciting day out at Fun World. But little do they know just HOW exciting it will be. So turn the page and join them in a great adventure.

Where's Teddy?

Wilfie and his teddy, Eddie, did one exciting thing after another...

and another...

and another.

They even went looking for sharks in the bay.

Then Wilfie noticed something was wrong. "AAAAARGH!" he screamed. "Teddy's gone!"
Sure enough, Eddie had vanished, but he'd left his shoe and his sunglasses behind.

Can you spot them?

The Search Begins

Poor Wilfie! Nothing cheered him up – not even a visit to the toyshop.

"I don't want this teddy!" he said, sadly. "I want MY teddy."

"You could try looking in the Land of the Lost Teddies," said the friendly toyshop owner. "Most teddies go there when children lose them. It's full of the things teddies like best." He opened the green door behind him. "And you're in luck! There's a train going there right now."

"Now let's see," said the toyshop owner, scratching his head. "Which train is it? I know it has a shape on the front, but it's not a star. And it doesn't have a green funnel. Well, anyway, the engine is red."

Which train is off to the Land of the Lost Teddies?

On the Way

The conductor blew her whistle, and soon they were off. Slowly they chugged through a magical world, past Spook Castle and Jelly Town.

"How many more stops before we get there?" cried Wilfie as they approached the Dinosaur Park.

"It's just the other side of the tunnel," said the conductor. "Not far to go now."

How many more stops do they have to make?

Which Way Now?

At last the train stopped at the Land of Lost Teddies. Wilfie gasped. How was he ever going to find his teddy here? There were teddies EVERYWHERE.

And there were certainly plenty of things for a teddy to do. Wilfie didn't know where to begin to look for Eddie. Then he spotted something that gave him a clue to where Eddie had gone.

What has Wilfie seen? (It's one of a pair, and Wilfie has the other one!)

Picnic Path

Wilfie hurried along the path until he reached a big iron gate. He read the notice and beamed. His teddy loved picnics. Maybe he'd find Eddie there.

Wilfie pushed open the gate. What a lot of winding paths! By the time he found a way through them, the picnic would probably be over!

Can you help Wilfie get to the picnic?

PICNIC TODAY
IN MIDDLE
OF MAZE
start at the
red flag

START

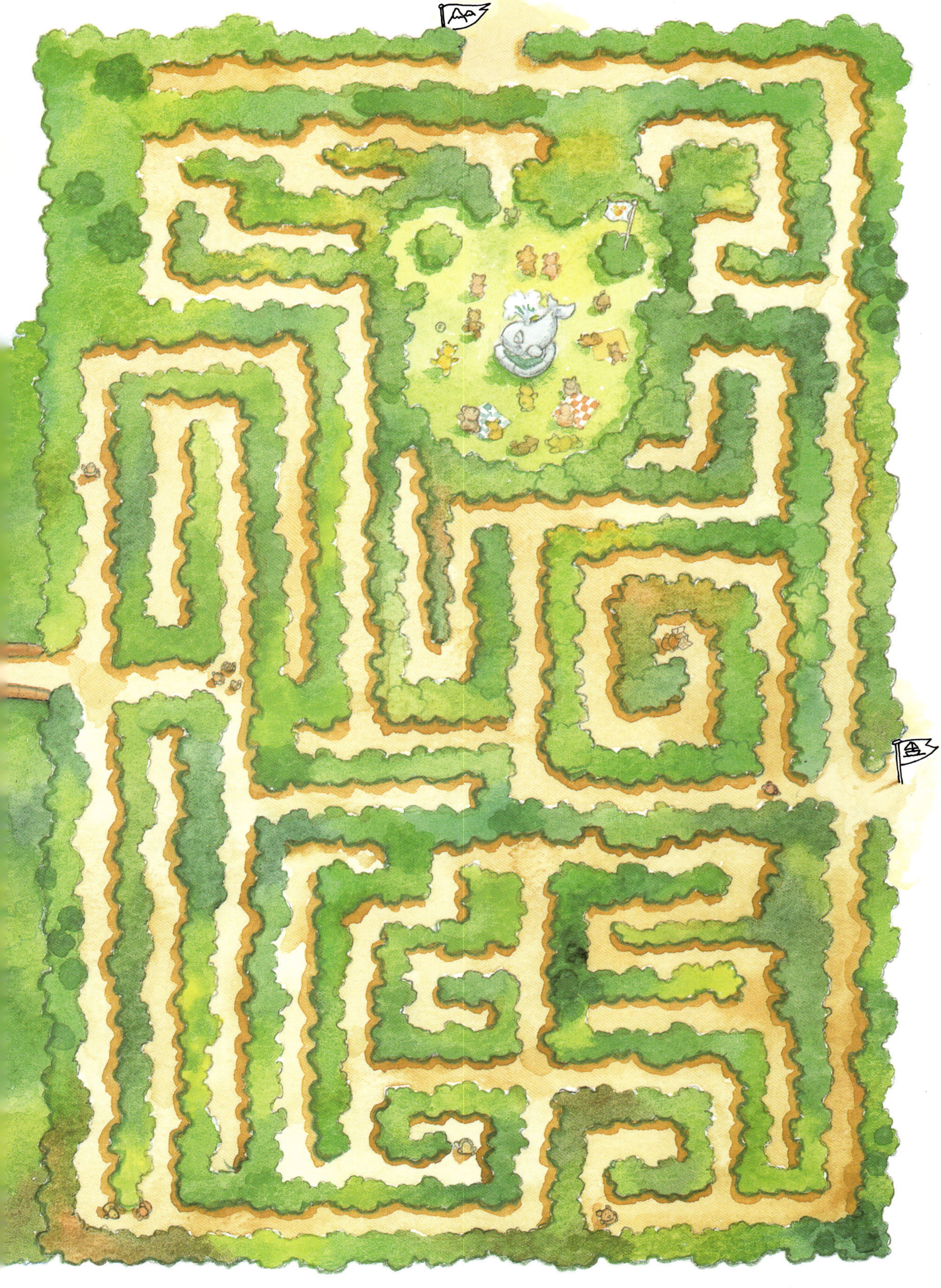

Teddy Bears' Picnic

It was just the sort of picnic Eddie liked. There was lots of food, lots of fun and, of course, lots of teddies.

Wilfie could see big teddies, small teddies, old teddies... but not HIS teddy.

He took out his photo of Eddie. Perhaps someone had seen him.

"We remember him," a yellow teddy said. "Who wouldn't? He had four slices of pizza, two ice creams, a banana milkshake, three strawberry tartlets AND the last slice of chocolate cake."

"Yes, and I wanted that too," sniffed a purple teddy.

FIND THE ODD ONE OUT

"We'll tell you where he went but please help us with our picnic puzzle first. We can't agree on the answer."

Which clown is the odd one out?

Bear Trouble

"He went off to the lake," said the purple teddy. "There's a short cut through the maze to it."

"But watch out. It's easy to get lost, and if you do, you'll be heading for Bear Mountain," the other teddy added with a shiver. "And we're talking big bears. VERY big bears."

"Oh dear," said Wilfie, as he went around in circles. "I think I must be lost."

It began to rain. It grew colder... and colder.

It began to snow. It grew steeper... and steeper.

OOPS! Wilfie bumped into something.
Something very large.
Something very furry.
Something like a VERY BIG BEAR.
Help! thought Wilfie. What's it going to do?

GROWL!

ROAR?

OR EAT ME?

The Bear Cave

The bear wasn't scary at all.

"OUCH!" he sniffed, holding out his paw.

Gently Wilfie pulled a huge, thorn out of its paw.

"Oh thank you," the bear said, smiling. "Now you must come to tea. Hop on my back."

What a ride! They galloped mile after mile through the softly falling snow. Wilfie clung on tightly to the bear's warm fur.

Then the bear stopped at the mouth of a big dark cave. "Welcome to my home," he said.

Wilfie soon told the bear all about his teddy.

"I've met him," said the bear. "He was going to catch a boat to Mermaid Island. I took him to the lake. He gave me something when he left."

Can you see what Eddie gave the bear?

By the Lake

After a big plate of buns and honey the bear took Wilfie down the mountain to the lake.

They waved goodbye to each other at the water's edge.

There were boats everywhere, bobbing gently in the waves.

"There are three boats free, but only one of them goes to Mermaid Island," said the boatkeeper, pointing at the pictures on his big board.

Which boat can Wilfie take to Mermaid Island?

Mermaid Island

Wilfie set off as fast as he could. At last, arms aching, he reached Mermaid Island. He searched for Eddie high...

... and low.

Found him! he thought.

But he was wrong. It was a merteddy!

"I'm looking for my teddy. Have you seen him?" Wilfie asked, showing the merteddy Eddie's photo.

"I think he went that way." The little creature pointed to the shore. "One of those pink snapping crabs just took a chunk out of his shorts."

Can you find a safe way to the shore without stepping on any rocks with crabs?

Another Clue

Wilfie searched left and right as he trudged up the road. It would be dark soon. Would he EVER find Eddie?

Then he saw a little pair of yellow shorts sticking out of a litter bin. They were Eddie's.

"Eddie's shorts had a hole in them," explained the teddy at the clothes stall. "He was very sleepy, so he was going to the nursery for a rest. He wanted a nice sleepsuit to wear. He was most particular. He wanted stripes, but not yellow. He loved blue, but not with red, and he didn't want anything green."

"I know what he chose," smiled Wilfie.

Can you find an outfit like the one Eddie chose?

Bedtime Story

Wilfie ran to the nursery as fast as he could. He knocked very loudly, but there was no answer. With a trembling hand, he pushed open the little wooden door. Would he find Eddie at last?

Wilfie could see sleepy teds tucked up in bed. He could see soapy teds splashing in bubbles. He could see story-time teds listening to a tale. And best of all, Wilfie could see HIS ted!

Can you see Eddie? Do you recognize the person reading the story?

Teddy's Story

Wilfie hugged Eddie as tight as he could.
"What happened to you?" he asked. "How did you get here?"
Eddie made himself comfy on Wilfie's knee, and then he began to tell his story...

A huge seagull snatched me up.

He dropped me as soon as he realized I wasn't a nice juicy fish.

I landed on a porpoise. He took me to shore.

I found a train station, but no one was around.

There was a box of blankets. I nodded off in it.

I woke up on a train. It was going to the Land of the Lost Teddies.

Then Eddie gave a big yawn.
"Now that you've found each other, it's time to go home," the toyshop owner said to Wilfie. "And I have a present for each of you." He scratched his head. "Now where did I put them?"

Can you spot the presents?

Homeward Bound

Wilfie and Eddie waved goodbye and boarded the train. Soon they were leaving the Land of the Lost Teddies far behind them.

Inside the presents, Wilfie found lots of things to remind him of their day, and best of all, he had Eddie back to share them with.

Answers

Pages 36-37
Eddie's shoe and sunglasses are circled below.

Pages 38-39
This is the train that is off to the Land of the Lost Teddies.

Pages 40-41
There are four stops ahead of them, including the one for the Dinosaur Park. You will find them circled below.

Pages 42-43
Wilfie has spotted Eddie's shoe. Here it is.

Pages 44-45
The way through to the picnic is shown here.

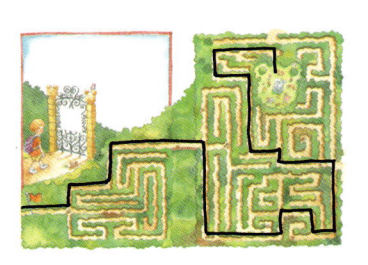

Pages 46-47
The clown circled below is the odd one out.

63

Pages 50-51
Eddie gave the bear his badge. Here it is.

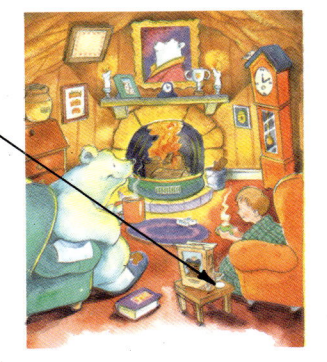

Pages 52-53
Wilfie should take the boat circled below to get to Mermaid Island.

Pages 54-55
The safe way to the shore is marked here.

Pages 56-57
Eddie chose this outfit.

Pages 58-59
Eddie is here. The person reading the story is the toyshop owner!

Pages 60-61
The presents are circled below.

MOLLY'S MAGIC CARPET

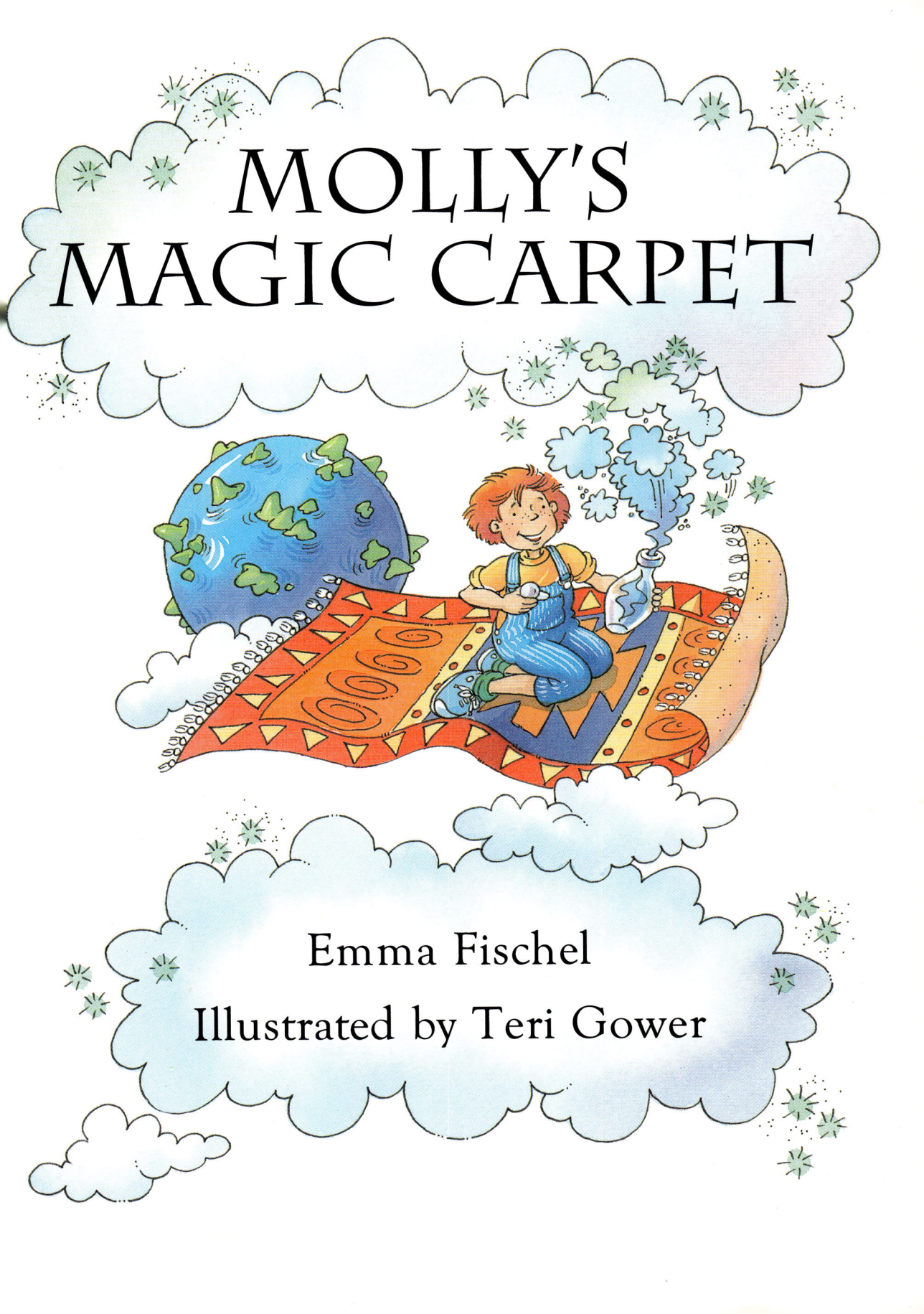

Emma Fischel

Illustrated by Teri Gower

Contents

- 67 Meet Molly
- 68 Molly Takes a Tumble
- 70 Up, Up and Away!
- 72 Wonderworld
- 74 Rocky Ride
- 76 Safely Ashore
- 78 A Strange Sight
- 80 Magic Mix-up
- 82 Molly Has a Plan
- 84 Flying High
- 86 Underground
- 88 Surprises in Store
- 90 The Spell Jar
- 92 Homeward Bound
- 94 Goodbye
- 95 Answers

Meet Molly

This is Molly. She lives by the sea.

Today she is on her way to play. But there is an amazing adventure lying in wait for her. Just follow her outside to find out more.

Keep your eyes open for clues. If you get stuck, there are answers on pages 95 and 96.

Molly Takes a Tumble

"To the rescue!" shouted Molly, charging down the steps. Today she was a brave knight, off to tame a dragon.

CRASH!

BANG!

WALLOP!

She went tumbling and landed with a big, hard bump.

"Ouch," she said and rubbed her bottom. "That hurt."

"Well, look where you're going next time," grumbled a little voice.

Molly jumped. Who had said that?

"Get your muddy feet off my back. You'll get my pattern dirty. And tie your shoelaces."

Molly was baffled. She looked around her. There was no one outside. But something had spoken to her. Something must be magic.

What do you think it is?

Up, Up and Away!

"You're a talking carpet!" Molly gasped, nearly toppling over.

"A magic carpet," the voice corrected. "Well ... almost."

It wriggled.

"The trouble is," it said, "I won't be a real magic carpet until I do something brave."

The carpet heaved a big sigh. "But I've been flying for days now and I still can't find a single brave thing to do. And time's running out. Soon I'll become an *ordinary* carpet — no voice, no flying, nothing!"

The carpet curled up at one corner. "Maybe you could help me," it said.

"I-I'll try," said Molly. And before she knew it, the carpet lifted off the ground and they were up and away. Higher and higher they flew, up into the sky.

"Where are we going?" Molly shouted. "Wonderworld!" cried the carpet. "We head for the big blue moon, then fly straight on until breakfast. Hold on tight."

Here's Molly. Can you help her find her way to the blue moon?

Wonderworld

Wonderworld! What a sight it was! On and on they flew, over gleaming oceans and rolling hills, over magical lands Molly had never even imagined. They curved and swooped through the sky. Molly felt light as a feather.

The wind rushed through her hair. The clouds flew by. Soon she felt as though she had been flying forever. "I never want it to end!" she cried.

The carpet chuckled. "Cloudworld, Spookville, Topsy-turvydom, Monsterland, One Mountain Island, all below us," it sang out.

Which island do you think is which?

Rocky Ride

Just then, the carpet started to jiggle and jitter. Molly clung on for dear life.

"I'm running out of flying magic," the carpet gasped, spinning down toward the sea.

The wave tops came nearer and nearer ... and so did a very large rock. Molly shut her eyes tight. THUD!

Molly opened her eyes. "We can hop from rock to rock to the beach," she said.

"*You* might be able to," sniffed the carpet. "But not me. I'm far too tired. You'll just have to carry me."

Molly rolled the carpet up carefully, tucking it under her arm. Then someone shouted from the beach.

Watch out! There is only one safe way to get here. Don't step on any rocks with crabs or slimy squids on them!

Can you find a safe way to the beach?

75

Safely Ashore

"Made it," gasped Molly, flopping down onto the sand.

"Unroll me, please," a muffled voice squeaked.

"Wow!" said the boy on the beach. "Can that thing really fly?"

"I am not a thing," said a small frosty voice. "I am a carpet. And a very special one at that."

"I beg your pardon," said the boy, eyes popping out of his head as the carpet spoke. "I'm Frank and this is my rabbit. Did you really fly here?"

"All the way," said Molly proudly. "Well, almost."

"Can I have a turn?" Frank said eagerly.

"A turn?" the carpet snorted. "I'm not a fairground ride."

"We could fly to the Candy Café," said Frank.

The carpet liked the sound of that. So when it was rested, they set off.

"There it is," said Frank. "It's blue — next to the umbrellas."

Can you spot the Candy Café?

77

A Strange Sight

Bump! The carpet landed. Molly gasped with astonishment. It must be carnival day. There were clowns and stilt walkers, jugglers and acrobats.

Then ... DONG! An enormous gong boomed out.

What happened next was the strangest thing Molly had ever seen. Everyone stopped moving ... everyone except Molly. They all froze to the spot like statues.

What was going on? Nobody spoke. Nobody moved. Nobody did anything at all. Then ... DONG! The gong struck again.

All of a sudden, everyone sprang back into life … and into a little trouble.

Molly stood and gaped. "What happened?" she asked Frank. But he didn't answer. He was looking for his rabbit.

Can you see Frank's rabbit in this picture?

Magic Mix-up

"What happened just now is nothing new," sighed Frank. "It happens a lot and it's all the fault of Mort the magician."

Molly listened hard as Frank started to explain ...

Mort the magician lives in a castle at the very top of the mountain.

He used to do nice spells. But one day he sent an invitation and all that changed.

Watch me test my latest brilliant spell! Come to the blue lollipop tree at 2 o'clock sharp. Love from Mort

The whole town turned out to watch Mort do his magic.

"The magic potion in this jar will turn any vegetable into ice cream!"

"I open the jar, say the magic words ..."

"Agga Zagga Doo Doo! And hey presto ..."

But the spell didn't quite do what it was supposed to. Little by little, Mort started to change before our eyes.

Everyone started roaring with laughter. Mort flew into a rage. He hated being laughed at.

"I'll make you sorry you laughed at me. Just you wait and see!"

Can you spot all the changes to Mort?

Molly Has a Plan

"So Mort thought up a brand new spell to pay us back for laughing at him," said Frank, leading the way to the Candy Café. "And now, any time he opens his spell jar, the blue clouds billow out and we all freeze to the spot. It's a dreadful nuisance."

"Can't you stop him somehow?" asked Molly.

"Only by taking the jar with the blue clouds in it," said Frank. "But it's hidden somewhere in his castle. We've tried flying up there ... but there is nowhere to land. We've tried climbing ... but he's covered the top in sticky toffee. We've tried everything we can think of ... nothing works."

Candy Café — Ices, jellies and lots lots more

Molly thought hard as Frank finished his story. "There must be a way up," she said. "If the magician does it."

"But he uses magic," said Frank sadly.

"Then so must we," said Molly. "A magic carpet!"

Quick as a flash, the carpet shot off and hid. It didn't like the sound of Molly's idea at all.

Where is the carpet hiding?

Flying High

"This is your big chance, carpet," said Molly, hugging it. "Now you can do something brave!"

"Well, I don't *feel* brave," it said in a wobbly voice. "But I do want to be a real magic carpet. So, let's go!"

"To the top of the mountain!" shouted Molly.

Soon the waving figures on the ground were just tiny specks below them. Molly and the carpet were alone in the big blue sky.

Up and up they flew. Past rivers that plunged into foaming white falls. Past forests of dark, densest green.

The side of the mountain grew steeper and steeper. The clouds rushed past. It grew colder and colder.

And all the while the castle grew closer and closer.

All the doors and windows are barred and bolted.

The secret passage to the dungeon is the only way in.

The Iffledffle plant hides the secret passage. It's blue with yellow thorns and purple spikes.

At last the huge castle loomed above them. Three magic birds circled around it, uttering strange harsh cries. Molly listened hard. They seemed to be trying to help her.

Can you spot the way into the dungeon?

Underground

The dungeon was stinky and dark. Slimy things dripped down the walls.

"Which way do we go?" Molly gulped. The carpet just shook like a leaf.

Then Molly saw a map. "This will help us," she said.

Can you find the way in?

X Way in to Castle

WARNING! WATCH OUT FOR FIERY DRAGONS AND SLITHERING SNAKES!

Dungeon Entrance

You are here X

Surprises in Store

"We have to find the spell jar," gasped Molly. Then they whizzed around the castle so fast, it seemed almost as if they were in three places at once.

They tried big doors and small doors ...

... stiff doors

... and creaky doors.

Until there was only one place left to look — in the highest tower of all.

But there was a shock in store at the top. Not one magician ... not two ... but three!

"Surprise!" they all chortled. "Only one of us is real. But which one? Guess wrong and – PLOP! – in you go to my pot of stinky slime!"

Then the three magicians started to sing.

> The one in stripes of red and blue
> Will plop you in the slimy goo
> The one in spots of green on blue
> Is not the magic man for you
> The one with yellow stars you see
> Is he you want, you see he's me

Can you spot the real Mort? (The song will help you.)

The Spell Jar

PFFF! Two of the magicians vanished in a puff of smoke. Molly and the carpet shot through the door and bolted it.

"You won that time," shouted Mort. "But bolts won't stop me and if I get to the spell jar first, I shall freeze everyone to the spot until Christmas!"

"Quick, look for a jar with blue clouds in it," said Molly.

Can you find the spell jar?

91

Homeward Bound

"Found it!" shrieked Molly. "Let's go!" Leaping on to the carpet, they soared out of the window.

Molly flung the spell jar up in the air. It hung for a moment then down it fell, faster and faster.

SMASH! It hit a rock and splintered into tiny pieces. A puffy blue cloud floated off into the sky.

"Spoilsports!" wailed a faint voice. "I'll never be able to make that spell again. It's gone forever!"

"And a good thing too," shouted Molly.

"Homeward bound," cried the carpet. "Hold on tight. It's a long way down!"

They played hide-and-seek with birds in the clouds.

They raced with shooting stars.

They surfed on the breezes.

They chased waterfalls down the mountainside.

Down and down they flew. And then Molly saw something she recognized. A tree she had noticed before that told her they were near their journey's end.

Which tree does Molly recognize?

Goodbye

"Made it!" gasped the carpet, landing smoothly.

"You brave thing," said Molly, squeezing it. She felt something.

"What's this?" she said. "A label?" She read it carefully ...

"You've done it!" she said, hugging the carpet tightly. You're a real magic carpet now!"

"Imagine that!" it said, twisting to look at its shiny new label. "I suppose I must be!" And it curled up at one corner with pleasure.

Then, waving goodbye to Frank and all their new friends, Molly and the carpet set off home. "I wish it didn't have to end," Molly sighed, snuggling down.

"This is only the start," smiled the carpet. "Who knows where we'll go next time!"

Answers

Pages 68-69
The magic thing outside is the carpet. Here it is, right under Molly's feet.

Pages 70-71
The way to the blue moon is marked here in black.

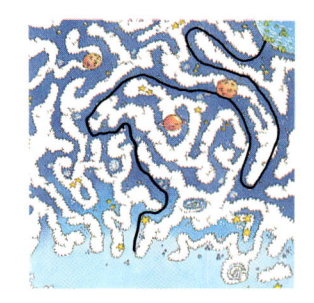

Pages 72-73
Did you know which island was which? You can see them here.

Monsterland
Topsy-turvydom
Cloudworld
Spookville
One Mountain Island

Pages 74-75
The safe way to the beach is marked in black. This is the only way that avoids all the crabs and slimy squids.

Pages 76-77
The Candy Café is here.

Pages 78-79
Frank's rabbit is all tangled up under the carpet. Here he is.

Pages 80-81
All of the changes to Mort are circled here.

Pages 82-83
The carpet is hiding above the sign for the Candy Café.

Pages 84-85
The Ifflediffle plant hides the entrance to the secret passage. It is circled below.

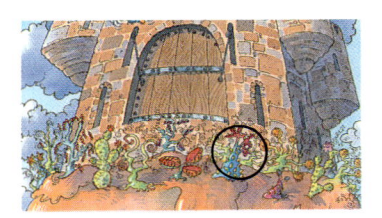

Pages 86-87
The way into the castle is marked in black.

Pages 88-89
The real Mort is the one with yellow stars on his magician's coat. He is in the middle.

Pages 90-91
Here is the spell jar.

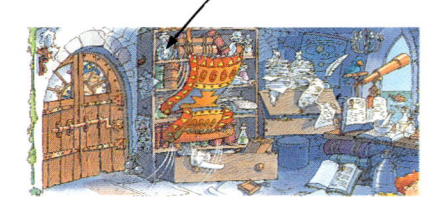

Pages 92-93
Molly recognizes the blue lollipop tree. She knows it means she is nearly back at the town.

First published in 1998 by Usborne Publishing Ltd, Usborne House, 83-85 Saffron Hill, London EC1N 8RT, England.
Copyright © 1998 Usborne Publishing Ltd. The name Usborne and the device are Trade Marks of Usborne Publishing Ltd.
All rights reserved.

No part of this publication may be reproduced, stored in a retrieval system, or transmitted in any form or by any means, electronic, mechanical, photocopying, recording or otherwise, without the prior permission of the publisher.
Printed in Portugal
First published in America 1998.   UE